STAVES

❖❖❖❖ OF ❖❖❖❖

SOUND

CompCare®Publishers

2415 Annapolis Lane
Minneapolis, Minnesota 55441

Grateful Member, 1899–
        Sparks of sound: reflections on wisdom heard at Twelve
    Step meetings/a Grateful Member.
            p. cm.
        Includes index.
        ISBN 0-89638-225-7
        1. Twelve-step programs—Religious aspects—
    Meditations. 2. Twelve-step programs—Quotations,
    maxims, etc. 3. Compulsive behavior—Treatment.
    I. Title

BL624.5.G73 1990
362.29'386'01—dc20   90-1966
                                                CIP

Cover design by Jeremy Gale
Interior design by MacLean and Tuminelly

Inquiries, orders, and catalog requests should be addressed to
CompCare Publishers
2415 Annapolis Lane
Minneapolis, Minnesota 55441
Call toll free 800/328-3330
(Minnesota residents 612/559-4800)

5	4	3	2	1
94	93	92	91	90

To my granddaughters:
Melinda Lu, Carol Ann, Linda Jean

Table of Contents

If I can stop one heart from breaking,
I shall not live in vain.
If I can ease one life the aching
Or cool one pain

Or help one fainting robin
Unto his nest again,
I shall not live in vain.

Emily Dickinson

Foreword

"Welcome to our world." That simple greeting at a Twelve Step meeting one evening years ago was the first spark of inspiration for this book of reflections. As the meeting began that evening, an oldtimer in the Program asked for a show of hands from those who'd had less than thirty days of sobriety. Upon seeing the show of hands in the group, this oldtimer simply said: "Welcome to our world." At the time, I had been attending Twelve Step meetings for eight years and I'd heard that greeting countless times. But at this meeting, I heard "Welcome to our world" as I'd never heard it before.

"Welcome to our world." These words are neither profound nor original. But on that particular evening, at that particular meeting—in my eighth year of recovery—God gave me the help I had prayed for through these words. In fact, this greeting seemed to me like the perfect answer to some questions related to growth that had been puzzling me for some time: how to meditate and what to meditate about.

Even though this familiar greeting made a sudden and deep impression on me that evening and answered some of my questions, I realized that I still had no idea how to meditate. I did know that I had a few things going for me that might prove to be helpful: college study, newspaper reporting experience, writing, and years of professional experience in the field of public relations. It was clear to me that certain elements of my life experience worked together to teach me how to listen effectively. Well-developed listening skills were gifts for which I was truly grateful. I guess you could say that I had a head start in my appreciation of "truth in words."

After the meeting that night, I began thinking back to how very indecisive I'd been during the days, weeks, and months of my retirement loneliness. Back then, I was feverishly seeking a purpose in life. Alcohol certainly hadn't helped me with my search. Now, after eight years, I finally realized that sobriety itself could do for me what no substance could do. At last, I could identify. What simplicity!

Driving home from the meeting, insight finally came. Out loud, I said to myself, "That's it, old boy. You can meditate on this world of recovery in the Twelve Step Program! There's a rich supply of truths about living—in recovery—a life shaped by honesty, gratitude, humility, security, faith, and trust.

And the good news is, you can meditate about all of these things!"

When I considered possible sources and topics for meditation, I couldn't help but chuckle a bit. Already, I had a big notebook filled with topics in quote form that I'd collected from Twelve Step meetings. The fact that I had started that book at all was one of those intriguing coincidences—"coincidences" that I've since learned were simply miracles for which God chose to remain anonymous. I finally realized that my collection of Twelve Step quips, quotes, and stories would supply me with material for meditation that would serve me for years to come.

I'll tell you how I came to collect all these words of truth: very early in my recovery, I attended a Twelve Step meeting held during the noon hour. At this meeting, a newcomer to the Program raised her hand and asked this question: "When do we get our memories back?"

Impulsively, I called out, "I'm with you, lady."

The room filled with laughter; that laughter told me that I wasn't the only one who needed a substitute for remembering. My own memory, sedated for years through use of an addictive substance, quickly lost track of all the "goodies" I heard from recovering people at Twelve

Step meetings. I'd hear these marvelous bits of wisdom, only to forget them long before the day was over.

So, even at that early stage of my recovery, I knew that I would have to do something to save the wisdom that was constantly coming my way during Twelve Step meetings. I figured I'd have to make some conscious attempts to do this until my memory improved sufficiently to retain the wonderful things I was hearing at meetings. At the end of that noontime meeting, I picked up a matchbook cover; on the blank space inside the matchbook, I wrote some key words I'd just heard at the meeting.

When I arrived home that evening, I used the notes I'd scribbled earlier to jog my memory. I then recorded thoughts that had come to me at the meeting from fellow recovering addicts who care and share. I continued jotting down things I heard at meetings and writing about these things later, long after my memory began to improve. Now when I look through my collection of quotes from Twelve Step meetings, I know that I'll always have things about which to meditate.

My personal collection of quotes from fellow recovering addicts has continued to grow since November 22, 1969. And all I had to do to build this collection was to "keep coming back" to meetings. So I continued to attend Twelve Step meetings—always concentrating on listening and learning new things from fellow recovering people. But attending meetings is never a substitute for working the Twelve Steps. Attending meetings and working the Twelve Steps are both essential elements for ongoing recovery and growth. We hear, we learn, and we get involved.

Filling a meditation book with quotes from literary giants and philosophers is an appealing and relatively common thing to do these days. Classic works are worthy of being quoted for they provide us with uncommon inspiration and insight. But in a book for recovering people, no quotes seem more appropriate and useful than those directly from the heart and soul of the Twelve Step Program—the loving, caring people who work each day to maintain their recovery.

The reflections in this book are mine, but they would not have been possible without the quotes that first "sparked" them and which anchor them here. These quotes have been collected over a long period of time. Some of the quoted material will be familiar to you, some of it will be new. While many of the original sources of these quotes are unknown to me, I wish to gratefully and respectfully acknowledge each and every one of them.

Herewith, my collection of quotes and my reflections from Twelve Step meetings. May they spark new insight and inspiration for all who read them.

A Grateful Member
Cecil C.

❖ *Acceptance*

> *"A world of difference exists between being resigned to a problem and accepting a problem."*

When we expect a reward or payoff for accepting reality, we are not accepting at all, but merely bargaining. And bargaining has no place in recovery. When we truly accept our *need* for a recovery program and the people who participate in it, we are putting acceptance into action and assuming responsibility for our recovery.

Those who are unwilling or unable to accept reality and responsibilities will not be successful in their attempts to integrate an ongoing program of recovery into their lives. One of the most important aspects of acceptance is this: *it is not a one-time task.* As recovering people, we need to accept reality on a daily basis.

" 'Maybe' in response to a request for compliance isn't necessarily procrastination. 'Maybe' can be a straightforward request for time to think over problems and situations before we fully accept them."

❖ *Denial*

> *"An addicted person is more likely to lie than brag about his or her use of an addictive substance."*

Treatment specialists in the field of addiction continue to identify *denial* as one of the primary symptoms of addiction. Indeed, addiction is the only disorder that tells its victims that "everything is fine—nothing is wrong." The basis for denial? *Stinkin' thinkin'*— the use of guilt and shame to encourage and accept dishonesty about personal behaviors. Denial sets the stage for self-pity.

We hear it said in the Program that an addict is probably not the last person to *know* that he or she has a problem...but he or she is quite likely the last person to *admit* to the problem. Denial ends, or is defeated, when admission and acceptance combine with surrender. Oftentimes, denial is replaced by willingness when the addict utters six simple but vital words: *"I give up! God help me!"*

"Denial makes the addict's brain like cement—thoroughly mixed up and certain to become rigidly set."

❖ *Love*

> *"Let us love you until you have learned to love yourself."*

Most people agree that of all the emotional tools available to us in recovery, love is the most effective and meaningful. The person who shares his or her problems within a supportive Twelve Step group is likely to find something very important there: assurance that others in the group will offer unconditional love as he or she learns to love himself or herself. Without love, we have no capacity for trusting others.

Love can be a great leveler in a world in which arrogance, selfishness, and greed threaten relationships between individuals, families, organizations, and countries. Love enhances character; love inspires good thoughts and gracious deeds; those who are able to express love are never bored with living. Love can blend the hearts of any group into a happy unity.

"The simplest and most effective expression of love is to wish someone well."

❖ *Miracles*

---

*"The age of miracles is still
with us."*

We need to guard against any tendencies
we might have to *rely* on miracles to solve
our problems. Perhaps the best miracles
for those of us in recovery are those that
move us to action and convince us that
we have the ability to be winners. The
best miracles also help us believe that we
can succeed, *regardless* of the odds that
might be stacked against us.

In studying the life of Jesus, one learns that although He performed miracles throughout the Holy Land, Jesus never did effect a miracle in the town of Nazareth. He had grown up in Nazareth and the citizens there simply did not recognize or accept his powers. From this story, and possibly from our own experiences as well, we see that miracles are most likely to occur when we have *absolute faith* that they can and will come into our lives.

"Fresh new purpose is often the outcome when we experience miracles in our lives."

❖ *Open-Mindedness*

"When we lock the doors of our minds, we keep out of our hearts more of value than can ever be protected by a closed mind."

Unless we keep an open mind in our associations with members of a recovery group and other people we come into contact with, we cannot hope to make desirable attitude changes. Tolerance with regard to the behavior and viewpoints of others helps to insure against destructive self-centeredness and grandiosity. Tolerance also serves to limit the growth and cultivation of resentments, jealousy, and envy.

In any group sharing, we can learn to express our views without dividing into "enemy camps." We who consciously seek to avoid preconceived ideas and prejudice will find that we can disagree without being disagreeable. The closeness we experience within a sharing Twelve Step group will teach us to really *listen* to opinions that differ from our own before we argue or take issue.

"When we realize that honesty helps us recover and tolerance helps us maintain *our recovery, we will understand that there is one short step from tolerance to forgiveness and love."*

❖ *Willingness*

> *"Willingness without action is fantasy."*

Willingness is the third element in a pattern of character growth some refer to as the *H-O-W* of recovery. The first two letters represent *Honesty* and *Open-Mindedness*. We need to approach the challenges in recovery with honest intentions and with open minds regarding the opposition we're sure to encounter. *Willingness* places us on the path toward sobriety. If we have willingness to accept reality and we act with honesty and open-mindedness, then even unexpected, unfamiliar barriers to recovery will not deter us.

We must be careful not to mistake *willfulness* for *willingness*. Willfulness is an insistence that things must happen our way and on our terms; willingness, on the other hand, is our preparation and readiness for facing challenges. Willingness helps us face and deal with our fears, and prepares us to make wise choices as we work to change our attitudes. When our willingness is intact, no problem will be too big for us to solve.

"Although we can benefit from being strong-willed, we need to use vigilance to insure that the power of willingness does not become willfulness and intolerance."

❖ *The Now*

> *"If we're busy patting ourselves on our backs for what we did yesterday, chances are good that we're doing nothing substantial about our spiritual growth today."*

Only by living in The Now can we close the door on the unhappy events of the past and lessen our fears of the future. When we fill our minds with positive attitudes today, we leave no room for negative thoughts about our tomorrows. Focusing on The Now can transform our thinking: instead of being fearful that today may be the worst or last day of our lives, we can focus on the possibility that today can be the first glorious day of the rest of our lives.

A close look at *this day* will probably reveal that it is the tomorrow toward which we looked with fear yesterday. When we focus our energies on the past or spend time projecting into the future, we separate ourselves from God, because He is found only in the present.

———————

"Reality reminds us that guilt is a product of the past and fear exists only in the future."

❖ *Attitudes*

> *"A productive attitude in recovery helps us see that faulty thinking can be as destructive to our recovery as wrongful acts."*

Those who develop an attitude that denies the need for a Higher Power are likely to sabotage their own efforts to find a source of comfort and help. On the other hand, a positive attitude that willingly acknowledges the need for help can lessen our fears of the unknown and lead us directly to our Higher Power.

When we have an open attitude, we will discover that the real benefits of some Steps in the Program come to us as a direct result of the spiritual progress we make in working other Steps in the Program. For instance, when we learn to focus on good thoughts about people we don't agree with, we are learning to accept the power of prayer.

———————

"Those who complain that they're having trouble with the Twelve Steps are perhaps really having trouble without *the Twelve Steps."*

❖ *Honesty*

> *"To recovering addicts, honesty is freedom—freedom from guilt and remorse that resulted from the denial and deceit that dominated words, acts, and thoughts."*

Serenity within a recovery program—as well as in life itself—depends upon our honesty. Most of us learn that we create pain for others *and* ourselves when we are dishonest. If we are to be true to our fellow recovering addicts and to ourselves, we cannot feel one way in our hearts and speak out in a different way. Genuine honesty begins within and flows out to touch those around us.

We cannot have too much honesty; on the other hand, we must never boast about our honesty. When we practice honesty in all our affairs, we discover something important: we choose honesty not because it is expected of us, but because it helps us build and maintain satisfying, clearer, more effective lives for ourselves. In Twelve Step groups, we frequently hear that honesty helps us recover and tolerance helps us *continue* our recovery. Without the capacity and willingness to be honest, there can be no spiritual growth.

"Honesty is not merely the first step toward character growth; honesty is character growth."

❖ *Humility*

> *"Humility is the willingness to be taught. When we learn the basic reason for adhering to personal anonymity, we have taken a vital first step toward humility."*

It is important not to mistake humility for humiliation. Humiliation was surely ours when we got into trouble in our lives because of our addictive behaviors. Humility, on the other hand, is freedom from self-centeredness. The man or woman who possesses true humility can, when apologizing, either stand tall or kneel. Humility is not a reward for recovery from addiction, but a reward for making positive and constructive changes in one's life.

Truly humble people hold their humility in their hearts, they don't have a need to talk about it or display it. Truly humble people are always available to give help and comfort to others. In fact, humility is sometimes referred to as "The Highway to Love." Humility impels us to lovingly care about and share with others without seeking recognition, applause, or anything in return.

"Humility is having patience to listen for God's will...and the open-mindedness to accept God's will."

❖ *Gratitude*

> *"Without hope, there can be no gratitude. To nourish spiritual growth along with serenity and security, we must cultivate an attitude of gratitude."*

Early in recovery, we learn that we cannot be simultaneously grateful and hateful. At Twelve Step meetings, oldtimers sometimes pose this question to those who speak of the horrors and unfairness of life's misfortunes: *"Compared to what?"* This query serves as a reminder to recovering people that the worst times in sobriety are better than the best times in addiction.

We really have no right to cry out *"Why me?"* about the unfortunate events in our lives unless we ask that same question in response to the wonderful miracles that characterize our sobriety. As long as we continue to say "Thank you" as an obligatory gesture, we will never find time to be truly grateful. Actually, just "feeling grateful" is not enough; we must *express* our gratitude by giving to others.

"Gratitude is the hinge on which our sobriety swings. Many recovering people living joyous lives of renewal remind us that gratitude is indeed the aristocrat of the emotions."

❖ *Laughter*

> *"We came to Alcoholics
> Anonymous to get sober, not
> somber."*

Through the years, I've noticed that many
Twelve Step meetings are positively *filled*
with the sound of laughter. The laughter
that newcomers to Twelve Step meetings
hear and participate in is perhaps as
important to recovery and spiritual
growth as honesty, acceptance, humility,
faith, and gratitude. Research data from
several sources supports the theory that
people who laugh often and manage to
find humor in a variety of life situations
tend to live longer, healthier lives.

Laughter can cement the qualities of fellowship and friendship that are key elements in a healing program based on sharing. Many recovering addicts learn to seek out people who laugh often and easily, as well as those who *create* opportunities for enjoyment. In recovery, we learn to laugh when we are alone and we also learn to find ways that will encourage others to share laughter with us. When you think about it, aren't many important life lessons learned when we're smiling?

"We can nurture laughter and recognize its capacity to advance spiritual growth when we tell ourselves—and truly believe—that 'a day without laughter is a lost day.'"

❖ *Involvement*

> *"There is a vast difference between action and activity. As with all other aspects of life, there must be moderation in our activity."*

We learn in recovery that boredom is nothing more than an inner need crying out for expression. Involved members of Alcoholics Anonymous are never bored. True involvement can be the element that dissolves our fears of other people and of the unknown. And the quality that makes involvement work is love.

Involvement begins when we know in our hearts that the first step in solving a problem is to tell someone about it. Unless we get right in the middle of our workable program, we run the risk of falling off the edge.

"Results are not the primary concern of the recovering addict. If we do the best we are capable of doing at any given time in recovery, results will become fringe benefits of our sobriety."

❖ *Vigilance*

"As a tool for recovery and sobriety, nothing can replace vigilance; it prevails over talent, education, and even genius."

• Vigilance makes us aware of a harsh reality: that life, for the addicted person, is what happens while he or she is in a dream world planning to be something totally at odds with his or her behavior.

• Vigilance helps us realize that when we're running from reality, it really doesn't matter what kind of shoes we're wearing.

- Vigilance helps us understand that the crippling anxieties that once haunted us were irrational magnifications of fear.
- Vigilance helps us become aware of just how important it is for our behaviors to be consistent with our thoughts and beliefs.
- Vigilance helps make the Twelve Step experience an off-ramp from the highway of insanity.

_____

"We never give up trying our best to prevail in the face of problems. The most tragic losers are those close to achieving something who withdraw their efforts because they are fearful of failure...and fearful of success."

❖ *Serenity*

> *"Not even contentment or tranquility can substitute for serenity, because serenity is a life force."*

As we mature in recovery, we realize that the sense of impending doom that haunted our years of addiction has been replaced by an ongoing sense of security. Serenity impels us to reject self-pity, for we come to know that there is no virtue, peace, or productivity in martyrdom. The peace of mind that serenity brings enables us to make a successful journey through any calamity.

The power of *The Serenity Prayer* is
a power available to us at any time.
We need to integrate each word of that
healing prayer into our lives so that we
truly know it and can use it each day.
Our look to serenity is always up toward
the stars rather than down at our feet or
back into the past. Many people in Twelve
Step groups say that serenity is "a pass-
port to the presence of a Higher Power."

---

*"Developing serenity is a journey
from pessimism to optimism."*

❖ *Turning It Over*

> *"Turning it over to a Higher Power refers to what we do with problems, inadequacies, character defects, feelings of guilt and shame, and whatever else impedes our spiritual growth."*

Many of us recite the words "Half-measures avail us nothing" without carefully contemplating the reality of that powerful truth. Why is it so difficult for some of us to even *think* about turning our deficiencies, differences, and addictions over to our Higher Power? Part of the answer to that question might be found in words that appear quite frequently in the book *Alcoholics Anonymous*, words with a strength and finality that could be intimidating—*"must," "absolutely," "never,"* and *"always."*

Completely turning over a problem or decision is a difficult thing for us human beings to do, because we tend to be fearful of change and uncomfortable with feelings of being out of control. It was our aversion to change that fueled our denial and prevented us from surrendering our problems to our Higher Power. *Recognition and acceptance of change* are key factors in learning to turn things over. The process of turning things over may be somewhat less traumatic if we remind ourselves of the most unchangeable thing in the universe: constant change.

"The act of turning over those things that are hindering our spiritual growth is one of the acts referred to when we speak of recovery tasks being 'simple, but not easy.'"

❖ *Prayer*

> *"When addiction—or life itself—*
> *has beaten you to your knees, the*
> *wisest thing to do is to remain*
> *kneeling and start praying."*

Prayer is vital to the spiritual growth that
enhances and sustains recovery.
But despite the importance of prayer, the
act of praying need not be complicated.
In fact, prayer can be the simple act of
hoping for something. Prayer is both
inspiration for belief and the end result
of believing.

Most recovering people agree that simply *conversing* with God is the best kind of prayer. But as with any effective conversation, *listening* is an essential element. Truly, meditation joins with prayer when we listen as well as ask. We will learn that what we ask for when we are on our knees is not nearly as important as what we do with the answers once we are back on our feet.

"Though it is not necessary for us to be on our knees when praying, reality tells us that when we are kneeling, we will find it difficult to be arrogant."

❖ *Listening*

> *"Had God intended man to speak
> more than to listen,
> He would have given him two
> mouths and only one ear."*

Sometimes it seems that the world is
full of self-styled orators who could serve
society better had they learned the
importance of listening. Improving the
ability to really *hear* what people are
saying is always emphasized in recovery
groups. In fact, the amount of pain one
suffers while recovering from an addiction
depends to a large extent on just how
"hard of hearing" one is in terms of
effective listening.

If we can learn to be truly attentive, we will continue to be successful students long after the early stages of recovery. Even as we read, we can *listen* for truths. Wisdom is the gift that often comes to us when we'd like to be talking...but happen to be listening instead.

"*Fulfilling conversations and truths are gifts of the ability to listen.*"

❖ *Being Needed*

> *"The most rewarding thing for a recovering addict in a Twelve Step group is to be needed."*

Sadly, when we were in our active addiction, we lost one of the most important things in life: *purpose.* Being needed by other people is key to the effectiveness of the Twelve Step Program. Quite simply, being needed restores in us a reason for living.

It is useful to remember the adage that "*We* can do what *I* cannot do." When we truly accept the fact that we are people who need people, we become very fortunate indeed. Twelve Step efforts we make will almost always be effective because our need to be needed is so profound and basic to our ongoing recovery.

"The need to be needed is a gift from our Higher Power."

❖ *Sharing*

> *"Sharing with others makes it possible for an addicted person to fully realize two things: that to be human is to have limitations and that to be limited in what we can do is to be human."*

The person who has only himself or herself as a teacher will ultimately regard his or her education as woefully inadequate. We can always grow and learn from our associations with other people. We find true sobriety only when we *share* what we discover along the path of recovery.

When people in our recovery groups share their experiences with us, we may feel that it is more useful to understand other addicts than it is to be understood by them. An overall attitude of give and take helps us better understand the gifts of life and recovery.

"When we share with others, we see more clearly the absolute futility of denial."

❖ *Choices*

> *"At any given moment, we are the sum total of every choice we have ever made. Hence, no choice should be made lightly."*

One of the primary freedoms we enjoy as recovering people is the freedom to make *rational* choices. Twelve Step groups are among our most valuable resources as we learn to make the best choices for ourselves in recovery. Our own experiences, combined with the wisdom of other recovering people, can help us determine if our choices are appropriate for a given set of circumstances.

Even if some of the choices we make hold various amounts of risk and uncertainty, we must guard against settling into patterns of indecision. There is nothing wrong with delaying a choice as we examine options available. But constantly wavering on issues achieves nothing; bad choices can be rectified with second chances. Common sense will guide us in making choices as we come to know the difference between positive forces and negative forces. We learn in recovery that when we make choices, we must have courage to follow through on what we choose and to use the power of that choice with wisdom.

"We are fortunate to have found through our Program a way to attain emotional security through making wise choices."

❖ *Shame and Guilt*

"Guilt is regretting what we have done; shame is self-reproach for what we have become."

The principles of the Twelve Step Program offer the very best sources of help for conquering feelings of guilt and shame. The positive actions required in working the Twelve Steps lead us from feelings of guilt, remorse, and shame, to the serenity of giving and receiving with good will. Shame and guilt begin to lose their grip on us when we admit, accept, and confess. Shame and guilt lose their destructive power in our lives when we learn these things: to share with others, to be honest, to make amends, and to have faith in a Higher Power.

Abstaining addicts usually feel shameful when they have slips. These feelings of shame about slips are understandable if an addict is depending on his or her will-power. But being dependent on will-power sets people up for failure and reinforces the belief that we are bad when we're unable to control our behavior. During our active addiction, it probably never occurred to us that we failed in our attempts to control our behavior because we were trying to will the impossible—moderation. And even though we felt remorse, guilt, and shame for losing control, we kept those feelings secret. The end result: *Hiding the truth from ourselves.*

"Guilt tends to make us feel wicked; shame brings feelings of worthlessness. Guilt results from transgressions; shame stems from feelings related to perceived shortcomings and failures."

> *"In sobriety, we don't stop making
> friends, we just exchange our using
> buddies for teacher-friends. These
> new friends respect us for what we
> are, not for how well we handle (or
> cover up) our addiction."*

As recovering addicts, we readily admit
what an addictive substance or behavior
did *to* us and we learn what long-term
sobriety can do *for* us. One important
issue for many of us in recovery may be
the fact that our addictive behavior began
in a spirit of fun or adventure. As our
addiction took hold, every drink, or pill,
or compulsive act made us feel all-
powerful—like King-Kong on roller skates!

In order to attain sobriety, we must dismantle our faulty thought processes and the complex alibi system that have so ably supported our addiction. In order to maintain sobriety, we must do more than attend Twelve Step meetings. Attending meetings is no substitute for working the Twelve Steps every single day. Sobriety reminds each of us to live in the now because, as old-timers in the Program say, "If you have one eye focused on yesterday and the other eye focused on tomorrow, you will be cockeyed today." Remember: *One Day at a Time.* The world record for sobriety will always be twenty-four hours.

"One of the great comforts of sobriety is knowing that the answer to every problem we encounter is there long before we need it."

❖ *Change*

> *"Before we fill a pitcher with fresh, clean water, we must empty it of any stale, dirty water already inside."*

In recovering from an addiction, we need to make basic changes within ourselves that will clear away the wreckage of the past and place us on the road to recovery. It is true that no one can carry out personal change *for* us; it is also true that we cannot change entirely on our own. Twelve Step groups cannot change us, but they can and do give us excellent tools with which we can work for change in ourselves.

The fellowship is filled with people who willingly use their own experiences to educate us. These helpful people encourage us to use Twelve Step tools to eliminate the sickness and powerful stinkin' thinkin' that have shaped our lives in negative ways. When we make positive changes in ourselves, we find the dignity and justifiable pride that can permanently alter our thoughts and behaviors. Our Twelve Step groups are there to support us through the process of change; our responsibility is the legwork...the action.

"When we refuse to learn from our mistakes, we are doomed to experience again the pain of our errors."

❖ *Faith*

> *"Faith is to the spirit what oxygen
> is to the lungs. Recovering addicts
> learn that faith is a constant
> companion of hope and love."*

Love cannot exist wholly on reason.
The presence of faith keeps love in our
hearts, sustains our new lives in recovery,
and insures ongoing freedom from
addiction. We in Twelve Step groups
learn that despair is the total absence
of faith. We learn in recovery that while
faith can rid us of fear, that same faith
will die within us unless we have a
sense of responsibility. As faith grows
in recovery, it becomes the partner
of miracles.

Spiritual progress makes us aware that if God could be seen, heard, and touched, we would not have the same need for faith. When life is positive and pleasant, faith can survive alone; when life is tough and there are no easy answers, faith calls upon trust for assistance. In recovery, it is our responsibility to make sure that faith never becomes an underdeveloped resource in our lives.

"We who are recovering from the stranglehold addiction had on us must equate faith with confidence. Faith constantly tells us that 'It will work if we work for it.'"

❖ *Excessiveness*

> *"It is said that an addict can use up a year's supply of anything in less than a month."*

Moderation is never good enough for excessive people. In fact, excessive people don't regard moderation as a positive attribute at all. The excessiveness seen in addicts leads them to believe in their hearts that anything worth doing ought to be done to excess. But, of course, more of anything doesn't necessarily improve results. We addicts tend to exaggerate feelings, opinions, attitudes, and emotions. When we excessive people are happy, we are the happiest; when we excessive people are sad, we are the saddest.

As addicts, our excessiveness took the forms of obsessive thinking and compulsive behaviors and, therefore, affected key areas of our lives: personality, productivity, consistency, overall health, relationships, and self-perception. But despite its pervasiveness, we need not *fear* excessiveness in recovery. As long as we can see clearly the futility and threats of excessiveness, we will be able to guard against it.

"Excessive people believe that if one of something is good, four will perform miracles."

❖ *Freedom*

"Answers will never be found if we seek them only in the dark closets of our minds."

Sobriety, gained through abstinence and the Twelve Step Program, brings exhilarating new freedom into our lives. No longer are we ruled by the bondage that began as threads of dependency and grew to the iron chains of addiction. Stigma no longer forces us into denial; we admit openly. As we come to know the real joys of caring and sharing in recovery, our freedom encourages us to give generously to others.

Our freedom brings new clarity to our lives: it leads us away from exaggerating and/or minimizing; it helps us see that we were born to dislike unhappiness and to hate being losers; it helps us become more decisive; it helps us confront problems; it encourages us to reach out to others for hope and help. In recovery, we are at last free to make rational choices that reflect our goals and dreams.

———————

"Now we are free to 'smell the roses' long before they fade."

❖ *Learning*

"When the pupil is ready, the teacher will appear."

Regardless of our age, profession, or education, we are in some ways *back in school* when we begin a recovery program in the Twelve Step fellowship. As we learn about our lives in addiction and recovery, we realize that there will be no graduation from this school, no diplomas marking the end of our education. In our Twelve Step groups, we mark anniversaries for significant periods of sobriety. But we're careful to observe these landmarks not as completions, but commencements—times when we recognize that valuable lessons will continue to come our way in recovery.

In our Twelve Step "classrooms," there are no restrictions in the process of learning: we can learn kindness from the unkind; truth from deceivers; tolerance from the closed-minded; and patience from the restless. We can show others the way to success by the way we correct our own mistakes. In recovery, life-transforming knowledge is implanted in minds that once were sick and hearts that once were sad.

"For recovering addicts, it is true that when we find a teacher, we find a friend."

> *"We will never be free of a problem until we've let go of it one more time than we've taken it back."*

We come to understand that there can be abstinence *without sobriety.* Our journey with our Higher Power is an uphill journey that is nevertheless joyous and free. But there can be no coasting when we let go of the things that kept us in our addiction. If we insist on coasting to sobriety, our journey will redirect itself... downhill. *Letting go is active, not passive.*

When we truly let go and turn our lives over to our Higher Power, we free ourselves from the fantasy world created by our addiction. Instead of living with illusions, we learn to live with *ourselves.* Despair lifts when we realize in our hearts that there is always a knot at the end of our rope to which we can cling as we call out for help.

"Even when we choose to let God steer our recovery boat, we still need courage to untie the rope that fastens our boat to a dock known as unwillingness."

❖ *Courage*

> *"It takes character to forgive others; it takes* courage *to forgive ourselves."*

Will is a word heard so frequently in group discussions among recovering people. But the *will* required to accomplish something is much different than the *action* required to accomplish the same thing. *Action requires courage.* And when true courage guides our efforts, we accomplish more and we feel more deserving of positive outcomes. By assuring us that very few things in life are impossible, courage helps us turn our dreams into possibilities and realities.

Experience shows us that courage keeps our emotions working for us in positive ways. We also learn through experience that real courage has nothing to do with indiscriminate risk-taking and reckless-ness, and much to do with common sense. When we believe in our hearts that a cause is worth fighting for, courage becomes our ally. Even if we're acting against popular opinion or the advice of others, our courage brings with it good judgment and prudence. With courage, great expectations *can be fulfilled.*

"Courage prompts us to confront *danger rather than wait for it to charge down upon us. Proper foresight prevents courage from being misguided or foolhardy."*

❖ *Don't Compare*

> *"Look for similarities—not differences—when you hear the experiences of other recovering addicts."*

It is important for us to feel that we *belong* in our Twelve Step recovery groups. In order to be part of a group, we need to *identify* with that group, not compare ourselves with other individuals in it. The only truly valuable comparison we make in recovery is between what we once were like and what we are like today. The details of our lives aren't nearly as important as our thoughts and behaviors related to our addiction. This is why the addict on skid row and the addict in a million-dollar penthouse can relate to each other in terms of what addiction did to them.

The recovering teenager and the recovering great-grandfather can find important similarities between them if they honestly look for "How it was" instead of "Why it wasn't." Addiction plays no favorites. Denial sounds remarkably similar in addicts of all ages and backgrounds: "Not me"; "We're not alike"; and "I don't understand you." Those in Twelve Step groups who react to the stories of others by saying "That never happened to me" almost certainly will hear this warning from oldtimers: "Keep using and it *will* happen to you."

"We will retard our emotional growth in recovery if, when listening to the stories of others, we persist in saying, 'But I'm different.' "

❖ *Patience*

> *"Patience permits us to determine if the answer we've reached is the solution... or just another problem in disguise."*

Without patience, we are so easily ruled by temper, anger, envy, and false pride. Impatience actually creates lethargy, for it causes us to waste precious time "running away" from problems, even as we're standing still. Patience, on the other hand, is the cornerstone of harmony. Patience prevents disaster when calmness and peace are threatened by a loose tongue or an impulsive fist. Through the steady, inspiring power of patience, many people are led to forgiveness and are able to remain centered during adversity.

When you think about the importance of patience to growth, consider how crops of the field and orchard mature. Consider, also, how baby chicks emerge naturally from their shells when the eggs are allowed to hatch in their own time. During a crisis, patience serves us best by reminding us that time is a faithful servant. Faith, peace, love, and humility are all subjects learned in the school of patience.

"Patience is not a 'grin and bear it' submission. Instead, patience is the acceptance of reality followed by careful, positive action. False starts and rash decisions solve nothing."

❖ *Being Alone*

"No person is idle when he or she is alone and absorbed in good thoughts."

Though many of the joys of living come to us when we're sharing with others, we'd miss many meaningful life experiences if we did not have time to be alone. It is during times of aloneness that we are best able to carry out our personal inventories and make plans for the future. Planning the coming day is only *half* the preparation for tomorrow; actually, we gain a head start on tomorrow when we examine the current day as it comes to an end. Both of these activities—personal evaluation and planning—are best accomplished when one is alone.

As each new day begins, we need to prepare our minds as carefully as we do our bodies. Preparation helps us meet and move through a new day as effectively as possible. Then, alone at night—silent and contemplative—it is useful to assess how effectively we have used the day that is about to end. If we wish to shift our focus away from our feelings of being alone at that time, we can meditate. Remember, we will never feel lonely during times of contemplation; when we are alone and look within, our constant companion is our Higher Power.

"By examining each day as it ends, we can weigh our victories as well as our perceived defeats. This process can help to strengthen our plans and our chances for success tomorrow."

❖ *Resentments*

> *"The most agonizing aspect of resentment is the continuous rehearsal of revenge."*

In and out of our groups, there will be times when we feel resentments toward other people. Occasional feelings of resentment are normal and more or less "go with the territory" of being human. We cannot run away from resentments, but we must not allow them to *consume* us. We are well on our way to eliminating the pain of resentment and resolving underlying issues when we speak directly and truthfully about our feelings to the person who hurt us.

Unloading an "injured ego" often results in an interesting revelation— that the person who is resented might be completely unaware of having disturbed another person's peace of mind. Knowing this may help free us from painful emotions. Resentments grow only when we permit them to grow while we sulk and allow our imagination to dominate our thinking. We can begin dealing effectively with our feelings of resentment when we ask ourselves "What is troubling me that made me resentful?"

_____

"Drop the last two letters of the word resentment and you have 'resent me.' Remember, when a person points an accusing or judgmental finger at someone, three fingers are pointing back at him or her."

❖ *Seeking a God*

> *"God is that entity about which a
> seeker for spiritual progress
> believes too much can never be
> written or said."*

Newcomers to Twelve Step recovery
fellowships are advised to search for a
God of their understanding. The search
for and acceptance of this Higher Power
signals the beginning of a special kind of
progress— spiritual progress that leads
to and sustains a free and joyous state
of serenity.

The act of seeking a God activates the willingness without which we can never begin a wholehearted search. But in reality, a search for the God of our understanding need range no more than fifteen inches—the distance from the mind to the heart.

"There are no half-measures in our search for a Higher Power. Going halfway in trying to find a God is impossible, because there is no half-God in the spirituality we seek."

❖ *Emotions*

"Emotional growth is the greatest force for keeping serenity from stagnating."

So much pain and suffering can be avoided if we learn early in recovery to reveal our true feelings to others without fear. The emotions we experience in recovery can prompt useful, life-changing discussions in our Twelve Step groups.

Every emotion we experience can be an important source of energy for us; feelings have power. But focus and commitment are required in order to channel negative feelings—like fear and anger—into productive thoughts and actions. Focus and commitment are also required to keep positive feelings—like love and humility—from becoming weaknesses because of excess.

"We will be most productive in recovery if we learn early on that we can, indeed, feel with our minds and think _with our hearts."_

❖ *Moderation*

> *"All negative feelings can be moderated. We can adapt anger, fear, pride, greed, and jealousy to protect and enhance our spiritual growth."*

Moderation encompasses reasonable restrictions, sensible controls, and realistic restraints. Unless our goals are somewhere within our limitations, we will be in constant danger of falling short or completely failing with respect to our dreams, ambitions, and even our sobriety. Disappointments quickly throw the immoderate, grandiose thinker back to feelings of self-pity, frustration, inadequacy, resentment, rejection, envy, and the all-consuming urge for revenge.

Moderation serves to level off the drive to possess all things and be all things to all people. Moderation can be used to weaken compulsive behavior; it can reduce the feverish drive to possess all things or be all things to all people. With a healthy attitude of moderation and a drive to achieve *balance* in our lives, we will not waste our time and energies in pursuit of that elusive state known as perfection.

_____

"Learning to live with moderation makes it possible for us to live comfortably with others—and with ourselves."

> *"Another milestone in recovery from addiction arrives for us when we are no longer affected by either criticism or flattery."*

Recovery makes a profound change in us. It's a simple change, but it is a change that completely alters our lives as we live them. When we are recovering, we wake up in the morning and say, *"Good morning, God"* rather than muttering, *"Good God, morning!"* In recovery, we realize that the shortest prayer we ever said—*"Help!"*—has been answered.

When we attain a state of comfortable, serene, and secure sobriety, we are able to say *"What has the Program helped me accomplish for myself?"* instead of *"What has the Twelve Step Program done for me?"* Recovery can be something of a game, but we must play this game to win and we must play by the rules. Rules? There's really only *one* rule in recovery, and it happens to be the same as the name of the game: *Don't use.*

"Recovery can be thought of in banking terms: Yesterday is a cancelled check, tomorrow is a promissory note, but today is money in the bank."

❖ *Easy Does It*

> *"We are successful in our Twelve Step recovery groups when we simply create for ourselves the ability to finish any and all projects that we start."*

There's an old adage in the entertainment industry that it takes at least twenty years for a performer to become an overnight success. That caveat reminds me of many newcomers to the Twelve Step Program who are impatient to set the world on fire with their recovery, right from the start. I believe that these newcomers would be served most effectively with an open and free-flowing discussion based on key slogans—*"Easy Does It"* and *"One Day at a Time."* Character growth simply isn't achieved in a day.

It is an old but true warning that haste makes waste. Think of it this way: if we try to climb a ladder several steps at a time, we're *inviting* slips, and perhaps even serious accidents. But remember, the advice "slow but sure" does not discourage consistent effort. As recovering people, we need to learn to solve problems as they occur, rather than postpone the identification of problems and project anxiety about possible problems in the future. *There are no express elevators to lasting recovery.*

"We risk losing valuable opportunities for serenity and security when we let tension and stress force us into trying to do too much in too short a period of time."

❖ *Pride*

> *"The last thing an addict swallows when he or she surrenders is not an addictive substance, but false pride."*

There are many kinds of pride, and they're not all bad. The Twelve Step Program teaches us that while pride can be positive, the kind of pride that "goeth before a fall" characterizes an unhealthy state of mind. This "false pride" is a manifestation of egotism, grandiosity, arrogance, and low self-esteem.

Spiritual progress is not hindered by pride if that pride is justifiable and if the recovering addict acknowledges the roles others have played in his or her achievements. In recovery, we always have the guidance, support, and help of other recovering people and our Higher Power. Truly, we never walk alone in any deed. Humble pride moves us to acknowledge our debt to others.

"True pride walks hand-in-hand with humility."

❖ *Mutuality*

> *"Mutuality is the kind of caring and sharing among recovering addicts that makes it impossible to receive without giving, and equally impossible to give without receiving."*

Addicts in recovery come to know that the act of sharing always rewards the giver. But in a giving-receiving exchange during recovery, the individual who receives help never is made to feel that he or she must return the favor. Sharing in order to help someone with a problem is carried out in the spirit that you can lead a horse to water but you can't make him drink... but you certainly can make him thirsty for the new way of life being offered.

There must be compassion before there can be mutuality. The real joys of sharing will never be known to people who are not capable of caring. Sharing at its best is an invitation to love that is never cancelled or withdrawn. If we want to give something that can never be wasted or wasteful, we give love. An act of true sharing always leaves behind something of spiritual value.

"In mutuality, our giving to others is never carried out in rummage-sale style. We do not give things that are worn or not working, and we don't give things that we no longer need or want. To aid spiritual growth, we give our most cherished possesions."

❖ *Progress*

> *"Recovery from addiction has no destination; it is a journey with many milestones. We learn to expect and prepare for the bumps along the way. Each feature on the road to recovery represents an aspect of spiritual progress."*

Progress is not an outright gift to us; we must make progress ourselves. Think of progress in terms of climbing to the top of a ladder: we'll never reach the top if we stay on one rung and don't continue moving upward. The rungs of a ladder are mere supports on the way to the top; to reach the top, we must continue our climb.

We will not make progress if we spend our time and energy resisting something we *don't* want, rather than working diligently to achieve something we *do* want. Some recovering addicts tell us that a good overall principle for living is the following: *"Expect the best—blame nobody—do something."* On our journey to recovery, any problem we encounter can become an objective in our progress. But we must be aware of problems before we can solve them. Those who continue to make spiritual progress succeed in growing up, growing deeper, and growing spiritually richer as they grow older.

"Spiritual progress is impossible as long as we choose to live only on the surface. Growth is the result of what we feel in our hearts; growth does not come from what we see in our mirrors."

❖ *Character*

"Aging is a necessity, but maturity is a choice."

Oldtimers in Twelve Step groups often tell newcomers to strive in their efforts to build character. Too often, newcomers are left with the impression that character is synonymous with reputation. Actually, reputation represents the collective opinion other people have of us; character, on the other hand, is what we are as unique, recovering individuals. We are not born with character; we develop character through patience, honesty, gratitude, pride, and humility. Fame and fortune are what we take, but character is what we give through an "outer show of an inner glow."

We recovering people must guard against confusing character with will power. An addicted person can no more will himself or herself well than a person with a broken arm can will that arm to heal spontaneously. In recovery, we often hear these words: *"It takes what it takes."* Character gets us to recovery and "It takes what it takes" to *maintain* our recovery. Character is not the sum total of the words we speak; *character is a force for living.* Overall, character is more useful than talent, and it blooms most naturally and beautifully in our contact with others.

"Character is a life force that respects truth, nurtures and refines willingness and spirit, accents positive action...and in doing so, inspires others."

❖ *Admitting*

> *"Admitting our addiction must be an act of unconditional surrender. When we place conditions or terms on our admission, we limit our progress in other Steps."*

When we admit our addiction, we realize that we are not morally weak people, but people with a disease. Some recovering people choose to accent the division of that word *dis-ease.* *Diseased we are.* We find that when we list all of the "coincidences" that brought us — as diseased people — to recovery, we begin to think in terms of a power greater than ourselves.

Admitting is an act of decision, but wise friends in recovery will tell us that decisiveness is ten percent knowing what we want and ninety percent knowing that we *don't* need addiction in our lives. Admitting is the first Step in emotional growth; the source of ongoing success is in the soul. When we admit our addiction, we finally surrender our "trusty" weapons —excuses and alibis. In recovery, we acquire tools that combat compulsion, addiction, and excessiveness.

"Admitting our addiction is not a one-time act, but a step of willingness we take every day of our lives. Saying 'I'm an addict' is a statement of our need for belonging and help."

❖ *Dedication*

> *"Dedication is something we must carry out ourselves...rather than directing others to carry it out for us."*

Recovery teaches us that we not only *make* commitments, we *keep* them. When a person has real spirit of dedication, the promises he or she makes are never hollow and the duties he or she accepts are never merely good intentions.

Popular wisdom encourages us to stay with a job until it is completed. When we decide to help fellow addicts in our recovery programs, we must dedicate ourselves to the task and never abandon our efforts along the way. Hope must be sustained as long as we can be of service. If an effort is truly worthwhile, we must give of ourselves to the limits of our potential, and beyond. *This is dedication.*

"When we voluntarily help others deal with their problems, we must be willing to do more than is expected of us."

❖ *Trust*

> *"We can never fully experience the God for whom we search unless we trust Him implicitly when He does come into our lives."*

Trust is closely allied with faith and hope in the development of our ability to achieve sobriety. And honesty intermingles with faith, hope, and trust; there is no such thing as dishonest or artificial trust. But trust should be cautiously placed; it develops only after careful consideration. Having blind trust in people we admire can make us vulnerable to betrayal and the bitter disappointment that results.

In our Twelve Step Program, we learn to trust God and we also learn to seek His trust in us. But unless we can trust our fellow addicts to show us the way to sobriety, we cannot develop the willingness it takes to sustain recovery. Trust is crucial when we work the Steps that require us to reveal personal things about ourselves. When we become more trustworthy ourselves and learn to trust others, we greatly minimize fears we may have about sharing truths of our addiction and recovery.

"Trust goes beyond belief: While we believe that a knife-thrower will not harm his partner in the act, we need to have trust if we are to become that human target."

❖ *Reality*

> *"Reality assures us that if an addict hasn't yet used for the last time, sooner or later that will happen."*

When we were in our active addiction, we believed that we could avoid the pain and danger of reality by retreating into a dream world. *And we often did just that.* When we share our stories with recovering addicts, we come to realize that fantasy can be more painful and dangerous than reality. In recovery, the decisions we make must be based on truth; we cannot cope effectively based on fantasy or guesswork. We discover that even though reality stays the same, our attitudes toward reality can change dramatically with recovery.

We are not always responsible for what happens to us, but we are always responsible for our reactions to what happens to us. We cannot find peace in recovery until we have surrendered to the reality of life. Reality tells us not to waste our time trying to avoid being what we abhor, but to focus on becoming what we want to be. Consider this in thinking about reality: it is better to experience a problem for which there is no solution than it is to know everything about a solution for a problem we'll never have to confront.

"Reality warns us not to look for answers in mirrors, but to listen to truths coming from our minds. We must not live entirely on the surface of our skin."

❖ *Kindness*

> *"When we are able to say 'I'm sorry'—not as an awkward apology, but as a result of spiritual growth—we will have learned the proper use of kindness."*

Oldtimers in the Program express honest and sincere concern for newcomers. It is understood by those in the Program that when newcomers seek advice or support, the responses they receive must not be false or in any way manipulative. Recovering addicts can ease the impact of "truth with love" by assuring newcomers that life definitely *does* improve when attitudes are permanently altered and spiritual progress is a goal.

If, for fear of "hurting" the newcomer, an oldtimer in the Program is less than honest, the results will not be productive. When that newcomer recovers and realizes that he or she was deceived or "humored" in some way by an oldtimer, angry feelings toward that oldtimer may well develop. Painful as it might be at the time, it is always better to be honest. Kindness is not related to flattery, nor is it an invitation to exchange favors. We express kindness simply because we have come to understand its importance and healing power.

> *"Many recovering people grow to the point where they express gratitude to people who once angered them by sharing with them a truth that brought progress."*

❖ *Fear*

> *"Fear is the catalyst that causes fear and also the cover-up for the fear we feel."*

Fear is our enemy only if we permit it to be. Both positive and negative aspects of fear are frequently discussed in group sharing. Fear can be useful in sustaining our instincts for self-protection; fear can prevent us from being foolhardy. But perhaps the greatest waste of time in our spiritual growth is fear of the unknown. At times, each of us is like the little boy who was afraid not of "ghosts that are," but of "spirits that aren't."

The free exchange of fears during group discussion can go a long way in breaking down the vague feelings of *impending doom* experienced by so many addicted people. Worse than fear itself is a dependency on negativism. A careful look at negative thinking reveals that it is actually a form of fear—fearfulness of being positive in the face of disagreement or embarrassment. We can conquer fear by doing the things we fear doing and gaining courage from our efforts and the results.

"It is productive when Twelve Step group members join together and list all their fears and the possible causes, then discuss them and seek solutions together. This is inventory at its best."

❖ *Friendship*

> *"Friendship is made up of
> one-third love and two-thirds
> forgiveness."*

Life without friendship would be an empty
existence. But, of course, in order to have a
friend, a person must *be* a friend. Through
experience, we find that the greatest
feeling we can have for anyone—whether
that person is a parent, sibling, neighbor,
coworker, or stranger—is to view that
person as potentially "my best friend."
True friendship has a beautiful, durable
quality resembling a miraculous flower
that continues to bloom in every season,
through all kinds of weather.

The first law of all friendships is sincerity. To break that law is to lose a friendship. There is never selfishness in true friendships. We particularly cherish our friendships during times of sorrow and discover that they can help turn grief and unhappiness into peace and serenity. Friendship can be one of our greatest assets in recovery. When we learn to forgive friends their errors and shortcomings, we can truly begin to forgive ourselves.

"If we are incapable of making and sustaining friendships, we will never be able to open our minds and our hearts to others or, in fact, to ourselves."

❖ *Impulsiveness*

> *"To say the first thing that comes to mind usually is the worst thing a recovering addict can do during times of conflict and controversy."*

When we speak impulsively and are ill-prepared, we are likely to become an obstacle for ourselves—an obstacle that can sabotage our wish to live successfully one day at a time. Impulsive remarks seldom pave the way for productive relationships and satisfactory solutions. An overall lack of restraint creates problems that frustrate most efforts geared toward emotional growth. We should remember the credo that "actions speak louder than words."

It is true that *no one* is always right.
Not one of us is sure of always winning.
When winning becomes too important
to us, then failure to "win everyone over"
may bring feelings of defeat and
discouragement that could lead back to an
addictive substance and a slip. All in all,
the slower, more contemplative way
through controversy and conflict may
ultimately prove to be the faster, surer,
and stronger way.

"When in doubt, say nothing."

❖ *Receiving*

> *"A Twelve Step group isn't just a program of giving. In giving love, advice, assistance, or whatever we give, we get back as much— or more. And to this we can say, 'Thank you... for keeping me sober.'"*

The belief that "it is more blessed to give than to receive" is certainly productive and positive. Still, it is important to remember that we cannot give without receiving. For addicts in recovery, sharing always returns many cherished results for which the giver is rewarded with gratitude. Giving and receiving represent a two-way street. One cannot exist without the other.

Just as there are miracles in giving, there are miracles in receiving as well. The ability to receive graciously is the key to lasting friendship. But in order to receive properly, we must be rigorously honest, humble, faithful, and trusting; we also must be unselfish; we must have belief; and we must have the ability to love without reservation. When we receive, our hearts must be open as wide as our arms.

"Giving is not really a responsibility; it is an opportunity to be of use at a time when we feel we have nothing to give. A thoughtful receiver makes the giver aware that he or she is loved."

❖ *Success*

"Success is a ladder that cannot be ascended with your hands in your pockets."

All too often, we hear someone's success in recovery explained as "a stroke of good luck." But those of us who discuss achievement within our recovery groups know that the degree of success we experience depends on the amount of good judgment, commitment, and dedication we use in working the Steps of the Program. While advice from others is beneficial, the *doing* is entirely our responsibility. No one can travel our roads for us.

While we know that some people are more brilliant or clever than others, we also know that *action* is the real key to success. Natural ability is of little importance to success unless we develop good, productive habits to support and nurture that ability. Success results from confidence and perseverance. We simply perform to the best of our ability, without grandiosity and within our natural limitations. We find that we can actually develop the *habit* of success.

"Success results from effective use of the abilities we have. We treat our abilities as practical tools, not magical gifts."

❖ *Truth*

*"Love without truth is
sentimentality; truth without love
is cruelty."*

Unless an activity begins with truth, it will
not progress successfully. Truth is the
medium of exchange in group sharing
and discussion. As the foundation of
knowledge, truth is the standard by which
the usefulness of our actions is assessed.
Truth cannot be bought, nor is there a
"middle ground" in the expression of it.
Things are either false or true; half-truths
are useless.

The advice "truth or silence" warns us of the harm that can come from rash or hurried judgments. Love and kindness must accompany truth even if we—as givers or receivers—perceive the truth as a painful reality. Group discussions will teach us that truth does no more than shed bright light on things as they really are. Truth never changes, but our attitudes toward truth *do* change.

"We should ask ourselves these questions: 'How can I trust someone who is untruthful?' 'How can I ignore examples set by those who are truthful?'"

❖ *Greatness*

> *"Some members of a group never know what is going on; other members of a group know full well what is going on, yet choose not to participate. Those with greatness are the members of a group who make things happen."*

Greatness is within the reach of anyone in a Twelve Step recovery group—provided this person has desire and dedication, and also aspires to ongoing recovery and spiritual progress. Biographies of great men and women reveal a common element that is worth remembering: the lives of real leaders demonstrate that greatness is not measured by wealth, influence, or power. True greatness is measured by character.

Unless a person has principles and lives by them, his or her life is only a charade. The spirit of giving is evident in those with greatness. In Twelve Step groups, we see greatness in our "Trusted Servants" and we read about those who *lived* their principles and, in doing so, developed the Twelve Step Program.

> "It saddens us to encounter people who have no belief in great men and women, for they are forcing narrowness upon themselves."

❖ *Honeymoons in Sobriety*

> *"The honeymoon—that period of time in sobriety when we feel euphoric—need not end abruptly if we take things in stride and always remember the H.A.L.T. principle: don't get too Hungry, Angry, Lonesome, or Tired."*

Recovery helps us regain physical fitness and emotional alertness. Most of us discover in sobriety, however, that it takes longer for the brain to recover than the body. Actually, after years of addiction, we are never fully and forever recovered. It is more useful and important to focus on the fact that we don't start using or acting out again than it is to focus on the fact that we have stopped using or acting out.

We cannot grow unless we put our emotional "houses" in order: We make efforts to stop trying to do everything in too short a period of time; we learn ways to deal with and reduce tension in our lives; we develop awareness of and gratefulness for small gifts as well as large ones; we handle our problems realistically. In fact, one way of staying grounded in recovery is to say of our problems: *"This, too, shall pass."*

"In our Twelve Step groups, we learn to differentiate between wants and needs. We reject fantasy and accept reality. Instead of spending our time analyzing the 'whys,' we utilize the 'hows.'"

❖ *Procrastination*

> *"We cannot know satisfaction and
> growth if we postpone seeking
> these things. Procrastination is
> the thief of time; in fact, a life
> pattern of procrastination may
> indicate that a person is not sure
> that he or she deserves the peace
> and joy of recovery."*

The habit of putting off action "until things
change or get better" is a treacherous
detour from the route of recovery. Delays
never make problems go away; delays only
make resolutions and successful outcomes
more difficult to achieve. For example: if
we postpone sharing with our recovery
groups our need for solutions to personal
problems, we create stress and misunder-
standing for the same people who could be
most helpful to us.

Avoidance of confrontation with reality often results from a fear that others will not understand our problems or perhaps will trivialize or ridicule them. And avoidance often leads to self-pity. Solutions to problems come from direct, expedient, and specific actions. We must remember that other people usually grant us "the right to be wrong," and that a change in direction always is possible for those with problems.

"Procrastination is the effort we make in trying to keep pace with yesterday."

❖ *Values*

> *"The most important possessions
> the recovering addict has are not
> things that can be held in the
> hand, but things that live in
> the heart."*

Identification of our values is one of the
most precious lessons we learn and share
in recovery. When we experience
character growth with fellow recovering
people, we can see clearly the things in
our lives that really count. Fortunately,
truly important things like peace of mind,
security, and spirituality cannot be taken
from us.

Even when we give away our best thoughts or share through action our finest efforts, these "possessions" stay with us. *The act of sharing allows us to keep what we give away.* On the other hand, things we give up in order to recover are things we really don't want or need, things we cannot use effectively and probably won't even miss. A pretty fair exchange, it seems.

"When we truly give of ourselves, the sharing doesn't stop with a single act. Those who receive pass these 'gifts' on to others, thus forming an endless chain of love."

❖ *Winners and Winning*

*"Winners make commitments;
losers make excuses."*

We recovering addicts live within certain
limitations, but we cannot win unless
we strive to utilize all of our capabilities.
A winner quickly admits *"I was wrong,"*
while a loser insists *"It wasn't my fault."*
Even though they begin in a state of
helplessness, winners in recovery
progress patiently: they move through
deflation and surrender, then on to
acceptance and healthy interdependency
with others.

We come to realize that pain is often the price we pay for growth. Just as wounds heal from the inside out, so must we rid ourselves of our character defects before we can present a new exterior. Winners do not pray for God to remove obstacles from their lives; winners pray for the guidance and strength they need to deal effectively with obstacles.

"Confronting addiction is like fighting a fire: we don't pause to analyze the possible cause of the blaze. Our first act is to extinguish the flames; only after the fire is out do we study its possible causes."

❖ *Awareness*

---

*"To recover, we must learn to
understand ourselves."*

In our recovery groups, we share
experiences rather than philosophies.
It is easy to quarrel with theories, not
so easy to quarrel with actualities. Self-
knowledge is understanding who and
what we are as sober addicts. The key to
self-knowledge? Learning to live with
awareness of both problems and
solutions.

Recovery is somewhat like learning to ride a bicycle: we don't learn by reading a book of instructions; we learn by *doing*. And once we learn how to ride a bike, we never forget how to do it. In recovery, we learn that anger is a detriment to awareness and that attitudes like trust are useful to us twenty-four hours a day. In recovery, we also develop awareness of the fact that once an addict, always an addict.

"Our awareness of togetherness and unity is sharpened when we join hands and begin praying in unison, 'Our Father...'"

❖ *Thankfulness*

> *"Being thankful for what and where we are in our spiritual growth is a constructive attitude that helps us defeat negativism."*

The road from a life of misery to a state of being happy, joyous, and free is actually a short path called thankfulness. When we are thankful for our blessings and our progress, we have come the distance from being selfish and self-centered. Thankfulness is a by-product of surrender and a statement of readiness and willingness to practice humility.

Because thankfulness embraces humility, love, and honesty, it helps us develop our spiritual consciousness. Truly thankful people know the meaning of caring and sharing, for they have consciously experienced both giving and receiving. With an attitude of thankfulness, we are no longer lonely or alone. Thankfulness signals the end of feelings that we are in sole control of all people, places, and things. Thankfulness also encourages us to let go of bigotry, guilt, hatred, and resentment—major blocks to personal freedom and spiritual growth.

_____

"To be thankful is an admission that we need love and support from others. Thankful people know they are not saints and can never play God."

❖ *Negativism*

> *"After engaging in so much
> negative talk about ourselves, we
> learn in our Twelve Step recovery
> groups that we are not bad people
> trying to be good, but sick people
> seeking wellness."*

In our Twelve Step groups, we're told
that when addicted people become
accustomed to pain, they find it
impossible to live comfortably *unless
they're uncomfortable.* In recovery, we
learn to look within ourselves to
overcome the negative attitudes that told
us we'd never achieve sobriety. In order
to break our habit of negative self-talk, we
had to replace our stinkin' thinkin' with
positive, constructive thoughts.

Negativism justifies feelings of unworthiness. An attitude of being "less than" encouraged some of us to declare ourselves "born losers." Many of us felt that we could never make the world accept us, regardless of what we did to improve ourselves. Negative thinking causes us to judge ourselves for what we think we *are* rather than to look at what we can become. Negativism can lead to us thinking, "I'm sick. Poor me...pour me a drink."

"Suffering requires no effort for an addict. As practicing addicts, we expected *to make mistakes. When errors or shortcomings didn't materialize, we found ways to* invent *faults in ourselves."*

❖ *Growth*

> *"The things for which I am most grateful today will be part of my life tomorrow, for I have grown spiritually."*

Growth is a personal improvement we must make *ourselves;* no one can grow *for* us. But, in recovering from addictions, we cannot grow solely through our own efforts. Insights based on personal experience are the most important things we receive from those who have preceded us on the path to recovery.

Attitude determines the kind of progress we will make in our spiritual growth. Efforts to please all people rarely result in growth; striving to be admired or loved by everyone usually brings bitter disappointment. We begin our growth by seeking to please *ourselves* through genuine caring and sharing with others. In time, we discover that character growth continues only as long as we are willing to work at it.

"Growth is not the result of obeying orders, but of heeding suggestions. We can see our growth when we have faith in faith, when we learn to learn, and when we have belief in believing."

❖ *Forgiveness*

> *"Unless we can develop the humility that makes forgiveness possible, we will never be able to cope with the feelings that make us intolerant."*

It does not take us long in a recovery program to realize that unless we can freely forgive others, we never will be able to forgive ourselves. Forgiveness is a crucial first step in our emotional and spiritual progress. Once the step of forgiveness is taken, it seems as though all subsequent steps to love, gratitude, humility, and honesty are easier and more natural.

Freedom to give ourselves a second,
third, or fourth chance to right a wrong or
perform a helpful act for another person
opens the way to spiritual growth.
Unqualified forgiveness—of others and
of ourselves—will prevent us from
becoming preoccupied with feelings
of guilt and shame.

---

*"Self-forgiveness is not sign of
weakness, but of strength. The
strength of self-forgiveness comes
simply from reminding ourselves
that if God can forgive us, we
ought to be able to forgive
ourselves."*

❖ *Learning To Cope*

> *"In coping, we are willing to take risks, but only if they are constructive and aimed at growth."*

If we don't let go of outside influences, they will continue to help us justify everything negative we have done, still do, and will continue to do. When we learn to cope with reality, we eliminate the externals, both past and present; we give up pretense; we stop doing things as we think we're *supposed* to do them; we stop playing roles because playing roles for too long a time permits those roles to *become* us.

Learning to cope with reality discourages us from becoming "blame throwers" at people, places, and things. To cope is to eliminate self-pity and procrastination; coping says to "Do it" because it can be done. Learning to cope also helps us eliminate impatience from our lives. Taking things slowly does not mean avoiding things. The slogan is *A Day—not a year—at a Time.*

"We need to be assertive in acts that help us cope with our efforts to grow spiritually."

❖ *Obligations*

> *"When we carry the message of sobriety to suffering addicts, we are obliged to not give up after the first mile of effort, but to go with the one in need of a second mile."*

Our efforts in helping others should always be carried out with the spirit of willingness to do more than is expected of us. No effort is too great or too small. Our total effort will be worthwhile even if *one life* is restored out of dozens of possibilities.

Our success in carrying a message of hope to addicts should not be measured by numbers of those who hear and respond to our words. Indeed, we must remind ourselves of our obligations whenever a need arises to answer a single cry for help. One success in carrying the message more than makes up for a hundred failures. We must also guard against feeling discouraged by delays in success. It is important to remember that oftentimes, the growth that comes slowly also goes deep and remains sure.

"We are not in the results business. Our primary task is to make the best effort of which we are capable. Any results will be added benefits."

❖ *Self-Centeredness*

> *"We are self-centered not because*
> *we think so much of ourselves,*
> *but because we think of ourselves*
> *so much."*

Many of us have heard in our groups that
self-centeredness is an inferiority complex
turned inside out, trying to impress the
world. Indeed, self-centeredness creates
and nurtures an insecurity that greatly
limits our spontaneity and joy. The
depression that develops from these self-
imposed limitations is sometimes
referred to as *frozen anger.*

We know that arrogant, self-centered men and women are often wrong, but of course they're never in doubt about their opinions. Spirituality simply cannot grow in the presence of self-centeredness; on the other hand, spirituality *thrives* in the presence of self-confidence. True self-confidence is the result of achieving and savoring success—success that we know is the direct result of our own efforts.

"Self-centered, self-serving people usually become so wrapped up in themselves that they become very small packages."

❖ *Problems*

> *"The addict's incessant search for problems leads him or her to lament 'What's wrong? Nothing's wrong— that's what's wrong.'"*

Early in recovery, the addicted person is prone to feel comfortable only when problems make him or her restless. At this time, many recovering addicts simply do not realize that if they ever got all their needed solutions together in a package of perfection, the bundle would be too heavy for anyone to carry. The notorious "slip" that sends recovering people back to their addictive behaviors *begins* not with that first drink, pill, or act, but with the addicted person's inability to cope with problems that already exist.

Most of the addict's problems result from faulty thinking. The negative attitude that prevails when an addict tries to cope with and handle problems is similar to this chaotic image: someone trying to thread the needle of an electric sewing machine while it is in motion. Actually, the most productive way of handling a devastating problem is to dump it all on the table at a Twelve Step group discussion meeting. We must be confident in our knowledge that there is no disgrace in having problems.

"If the addict who fails to find sobriety actually walked like he or she thought, he or she would fall flat after only a couple of steps."

❖ *Lifeboat Built for All Ages*

"There is no generation gap in Twelve Step Programs. Each person in the group, regardless of age, has the same goal: sobriety, and the spiritual progress that makes that sobriety serene and secure."

The elder and the preteen attending the same Twelve Step group meeting can both relate to the same issues in their search for serenity: *the seriousness of addiction and the necessity for emotional growth in abstinence.* Elders attending Twelve Step meetings are never made to feel that "I'm too old" or "it's too late." Preteens attending Twelve Step meetings are never made to feel that "I'm too young to be addicted."

146

Think of a Twelve Step recovery group as a group of people who survive in a lifeboat following a shipwreck. Each individual has roughly the same chance for survival. An older person has as much chance to "make it to solid, lasting recovery" as a younger person who has been addicted for less than a year. Just as people of all ages die of substance abuse, so do people of all ages recover from addiction and grow spiritually.

"In Twelve Step group meetings, newcomers benefit by listening to the experiences of oldtimers, and oldtimers find renewal in the hope expressed by newcomers."

❖ *Hitting Bottom*

> *"We hit bottom when we stop digging for excuses, alibis, and loopholes in order to avoid admitting and accepting our addiction and our need for a recovery program."*

Regardless of where we are when we hit bottom, the only direction toward recovery is up. Already, we've gone all the way to hell and made a U-turn. In the early days of Twelve Step Programs, recovering addicts somewhat kiddingly told newcomers that if they still owned a watch, they hadn't hit bottom yet.

The truth is that many addicts find solid sobriety without first losing their homes, families, or bank accounts. Hitting bottom is relative; each person determines that unforgettable place for himself or herself. But no matter where a person is when he or she hits bottom—on skid row or on a luxury ocean cruise—it is that bottoming-out experience that often leads directly to admitting and accepting. The bottom is the point where the addict stops allowing life to happen *to* him or her and begins making life happen *for* him or her.

> "The bottom for any addict is that point where he or she surrenders to the reality that his or her addictive behavior has become uncontrollable. This is the point where denial ends and truth takes over."

> *"Twelve Step recovery meetings*
> *represent a chance for losers to*
> *come together to talk about*
> *their winnings."*

Newcomers to Twelve Step meetings are told to keep coming back so that they can see for themselves what happens to those in the Program who *stop* coming back. Newcomers who are still in denial are told this at meetings: "Don't be afraid to mingle with us; addiction is a disease, but it isn't contagious." Oldtimers tell us that it's better for a person to sit in a hard chair at a Twelve Step meeting *wondering* if he or she is addicted than it is for him or her to slouch in an overstuffed chair at home—using an addictive substance and *acting out* his or her addiction.

While Twelve Step meetings are serious and sometimes intense, they aren't sad. There is much to be learned at meetings, even when one isn't in the *mood* to learn. In fact, many of us have heard it said that a person attending a Twelve Step meeting gathers wisdom just as a man in a blue serge suit gathers floss as he walks through a cotton field in bloom.

"When a newcomer or interested visitor at a Twelve Step meeting observes the joyousness and serenity of the men and women there, he or she may conclude: 'I won't ever have to ask God to bless these people because he already has done that.'"

❖ *Beauty*

> *"Beauty is not a gift, but an attainment. Beautiful roses will never appear in our gardens unless we work hard for them and perform life-sustaining tasks of weeding, watering, hoeing, feeding, pruning, and spraying."*

We do not need mirrors or magnifiers to see the inner glow of beauty in people who have come from despair into a world of constant, vigilant, and serene sobriety. The beauty enjoyed by recovering addicts does not come miraculously like manna from Heaven, but through the tasks of attaining and maintaining recovery.

Beauty is seen, but also *experienced.*
In recovery, we begin to see beauty as a
promise of serenity. The words *beauty*
and *beautiful* are among the most useful
we'll ever contemplate or utter if we hope
to continue making spiritual progress.
These words describe not only the
exteriors of people, places, and things,
but the joys and serenity that are to be
found within. In its most basic form,
beauty is love and service looking at
themselves in a mirror.

----

*"When we cannot find beauty in
our solutions, we will know that
our answers are wrong."*

❖ *Communicating*

"*Controversy should not be part of our Twelve Step group sharing because it signifies divisiveness, and that leads to disunity. We can disagree without being disagreeable.*"

Learning why we don't agree with each other regarding certain subjects is an integral part of our spiritual progress. We are told to always utilize and seldom analyze. This advice permits us to give others the right to be wrong and—harder yet for the headstrong—the right to be right.

In our Twelve Step groups, we learn to be tolerant of the opinions of others, but we don't dodge difficult problems. Calling our Program simple does not mean that it is without challenge or difficulty. In recovery, we all agree that the promises of sobriety come only if we work for them. In our Twelve Step groups, we learn and grow spiritually during healthy exchanges that often reveal dramatic differences of opinion. We agree that we are not a debating society, but simply a fellowship of people with different backgrounds, experiences, and points of view.

"If everyone in Twelve Step recovery groups got to sobriety in exactly the same way and proceeded to think and act on the same wavelength, we might become bored to the point of taking our problems elsewhere."

❖ *Bright Viewpoint*

*"An optimist sees a light at the end
of the tunnel of recovery and
knows it's not the headlight of
another destructive force."*

Even when we're actively trying to
improve the quality of our lives in
recovery, we still are impatient and
despairing at times. Many recovering
addicts seek comfort from others when
frustration threatens to affect their goals
for recovery and life. But it's always
frustrating to discover that there are
people who, though well-meaning, don't
understand or appreciate our problems,
our Program, or our goals.

For those seeking spiritual growth, it is useful to remember the object lesson of an experienced mountain climber: during his journey, he rarely looks up the mountain to see how much further he must climb to reach the summit. Instead, each time the climber rests on his journey, he looks down at the place where he started. The vast, inspiring vistas this mountain climber sees when resting show him what he already has achieved.

"We cannot expect everyone in our lives to be as enthusiastic as we are about our goals. But for the sake of our goals, we must not allow the attitudes of others to affect our commitment and enthusiasm."

❖ *Obsessive Emotions*

"As recovering addicts, we must guard against obsessiveness in all things, including our emotions."

Obsessiveness has many names—excessiveness, compulsion, impatience, lack of restraint, hyperactivity, lack of will power, and greed. When we permit obsessiveness to drive our thoughts and activities, we eventually exhaust our inner resources. Obsessive people often express uncontrolled covetousness; they want their share, and more, of everything—good and bad.

Obsessive people tend to be overbearing in their efforts to thrust sobriety upon reluctant newcomers; they also tend to overdo love in a way best expressed by "you're killing him/her with kindness." Most frustrating for others, perhaps, is the tendency for obsessive people to act on the belief that nothing is too good not to be redone. To obsessive "fix-it" attitudes among newcomers, oldtimers in the Program often say *If it works, don't fix it.*

"Excessive thinking can range in extremes from humility to arrogance, from self-pity to egotism, from low self-worth to grandiosity, from hatred to love."

❖ *Self-Pity*

> *"Self-pity is like a wet diaper. For a time it is comfortable, but then it begins to stink."*

As addicts, we wasted countless hours of our lives feeling sorry for ourselves: we believed that we were losers; we believed that no one liked us and never would, no matter how hard we worked to accommodate or please; we believed that the world owed us an enormous debt and was refusing to pay up; we feared the known and the unknown; we wanted things to happen *for* us; we never created or seized our own opportunities; we worried excessively.

When we finally *did* let go of self-pity, we did not do so willingly. If we didn't give up our self-pity kicking and screaming, we gave it up mighty reluctantly. In our Program we learned that self-pity had to go or *we'd* end up going. Words like these helped many of us "hang in there" until self-pity lost its appeal: *"Don't give up before the miracles can happen."*

"Self-pity is a form of anxiety. Recognizing its menacing qualities can help us find sobriety."

❖ *Our Own Worst Enemy*

"The choice is ours to make: each of us can be either our own worst enemy or our own best friend."

At Twelve Step meetings, we often hear recovering people admit that when they were actively addicted, they were their own worst enemies. These same people are fortunate to be able to add this postscript to their stories: *"But today, I like myself and I'm a good friend to myself."* After being characteristically cruel to ourselves as addicts, we find in the Twelve Step Program golden opportunities to be good to ourselves and to make life-transforming changes as well.

It is so true that we are capable of being our most serious problem or our very best solution. Our Twelve Step Program offers us clear choices in self-evaluation that can lead us to new beliefs, attitudes, and actions: we can stop hating ourselves or start liking ourselves; we can put ourselves down or lift ourselves up; we can be our own detractors or our own supporters; we can be negative or positive.

"Because the problems we had when we were acting out our addiction were self-induced, one could say that our potential for recovery depends on how good we are to ourselves."

❖ *Envy and Jealousy*

> *"Envy and jealousy stem from feelings of inadequacy and are abetted by a diminished trust in God. Envy and jealousy flourish with self-centeredness."*

The *Big Book* informs us that among the greatest enemies of the recovering addict are envy and jealousy. Envy has its roots in feelings of being "less than" other people. Naturally, these feelings relate to a basic lack of self-worth. We are jealous of others primarily because we're disappointed that we are unable to match their achievements. Small wonder that envy is called the "green monster" of emotions.

Envy is always intolerant. Harmful jealousy cannot contribute in any way to spiritual progress, because at its foundation is the degradation of those we feel are more successful than we are. As newcomers to Twelve Step Programs, we were told that envy is a sore eye that cannot tolerate light and that jealousy is a commitment entirely devoid of graciousness. Ultimately, jealousy and envy shatter every shred of our self-worth. The solution? Changing our attitudes and becoming willing to work diligently for what we want.

"Envy can be beneficial if what we envy are the good things in others and the realization that they have earned them. We can envy winners with love."

❖ *People-Pleasing*

> *"People-pleasers spend money they don't have —to buy things they don't need —to impress people they don't like."*

Pleasing others by doing affirming, supportive, worthwhile things for them— and not expecting anything in return—is healthy people-pleasing. But addicted people often strive compulsively to please those who they believe are most likely to acknowledge their actions with rewards, assistance, and reciprocal acts. People-pleasers want success *given* to them because they're not willing to risk trying for themselves or because they perceive that success is beyond their ability to earn it. Ultimately, the compulsive people-pleaser fuels his or her own feelings of unworthiness and inferiority.

Compulsive people-pleasers characteristically fail in loving relationships. True loving feelings for another person cannot grow until one has learned that real love is never given with the expectation of reward or reciprocity. Seeking the attention and approval of others sets us up for suspicion, jealousy, and resentment—particularly when compliments don't come our way as a result. Actually, mere compliments are too short-lived and fragile for compulsive people-pleasers. In recovery, we learn that approval comes when we make genuine, consistent efforts to *be* someone, rather than to do something ingratiating for another person.

"We must learn to appreciate our critics. People who fail to applaud us are not enemies; in fact, they may be our most helpful friends."

❖ We "Almost" People

> *"As addicts, we lived our own conception of happiness by* almost *achieving. In recovery, however,* almost success *is not enough."*

During our most frustrating times of using, how often did we try to console ourselves by saying, "I *almost* made it to the end of the day without using"? We believed that *almost* was a clear indication that we were coming closer to sobriety. Somehow, we convinced ourselves that falling just a *bit* short of abstinence was cause for commendation. With this attitude of denial, we never accepted the fact that these near-misses were actually complete failures.

In our denial, we simply didn't realize
that our addiction was getting worse, not
better, when each day became another
cycle of compulsive behavior. False pride
was our explanation for each failure to rise
above *almost.* We blamed bad luck and
the betrayals of others for our *nearlies.* At
that time, most of us weren't familiar with
the Twelve Step Program, so we hadn't
heard that "Half-measures avail us
nothing." If we'd had access at that time to
the slogan "Easy Does It," we probably
would have welcomed that as an alibi.

---

*"With our acceptance of near-wins
in terms of sobriety, we were
always surprised and
disappointed when our vow that
'Today will be different' was never
carried out."*

❖ *Slowly But Surely*

> *"Patience is key to practicing the advice 'Don't push.' If put into practice, those words of advice can be a very effective warning for compulsive people who always want too much, too soon."*

Taking spiritual progress as it comes to us in recovery is a sure-fire cure for those of us who are tempted to *push* for results. But a comfortable rate of steady growth is frequently regarded as unsatisfactory by those who want progress on their own terms. Impatient newcomers are often told that "The only thing you can have completely on your own terms is the purchase of the *Big Book!*"

Attempting to grow spiritually at high speed can disrupt a natural progression to serenity and security. Even the most excessive of us will be frustrated by impatience. The inner pressure that we exert on ourselves often makes our observable efforts offensive to others. The greater the pressure to achieve results, the greater the impulse to overdo efforts.

"Steady growth in recovery quiets the impulse to want far more than our capabilities and limitations can tolerate."

❖ *Value of Time*

> *"Time is the best tool for altering our attitudes. There are moments when just 'playing for time' will be enough to avert or survive a crisis."*

Rest, diversion, and "time off" can *prepare* us to face the challenges of living. During group sharing, we can use our time effectively through positive discussion and sharing with others. Time can also be an ally when we are impelled toward rage. When anger is slow-burning, we have some time to decide whether or not the impending fury will be worth the pain that may result.

Of course, living in *the now* is a primary goal for recovering addicts and other healthy people. But with priorities, planning, and careful use of time, the future can be prepared for even as we focus on living one day at a time.

"Remember, God gives us all the time we want to 'play God'— as long as we can stand it. Ultimately, we'll be relieved to return the job to our Higher Power."

❖ *Complacency*

> *"It is oftentimes more difficult to cope with success than with failure. Adversity can be a less complex problem than good fortune."*

Within every fellowship of recovering people there are remarkable success stories that generate great pride for achievers and their admirers. But pride must be justified. Those who succeed always face the hazard of developing an attitude of smug satisfaction, along with the erroneous belief that "I've got it made." *I've got it made*—this thought characterizes complacency, a potent enemy of ongoing recovery and growth. Those who succeed in sustaining recovery and spiritual growth are not content to "rest on their laurels."

We must be aware that vigilance is required if we are to hold our own in one-day-at-a-time living. When we are alert to the importance of holding onto, understanding, and nurturing our gains and successes rather than *gloating* over them or taking them for granted, we are more likely to avoid disappointments and setbacks. Complacency is the enemy within that proclaims "I've got it made." And the first cousin of complacency? *Carelessness.* Both complacency and carelessness can lead us to slips before we're even aware of what is happening.

"It would be relatively easy to begin feeling as though we had it made if we truly believed that all we had to do was accept reality, then relax. We do learn, however, that maintaining recovery signals the beginning of real growth."

❖ *Being Ourselves*

> *"No two people in a Twelve Step group are the same. In a recovery group, as in life, each person is a separate individual."*

Though there may be some striking similarities between individuals in a Twelve Step group, we must always remember this: *the group is made up of separate individuals;* there are no duplicates. Of course, our lives are influenced forever by those with whom we share in a recovery group. But even as we grow spiritually and share with others, we cannot think for others and they cannot think for us. Learning this basic truth about separateness in the Program and in life will help us maintain our individuality as we share problems and solutions with others.

We never force our ideas on other people; we simply offer whatever information we have with love. An individual can best serve a recovery group by relating his or her own experiences and sharing the lessons he or she has learned from that reality. Each person in a recovery group accepts data and interpretations from others, then adapts that information for his or her own needs. For each individual man and woman in recovery, "It takes what it takes."

"It is not possible to be true to ourselves if we envy others their knowledge and try to imitate them. We can only pursue what we feel is best for us personally."

❖ *Taking Aim*

> *"To be told that one is blameless is not a compliment at all. Only those who attempt nothing can be completely blameless."*

In sharing with others in our Twelve Step recovery groups, we should not be timid about discussing our goals—both short-range and long-term. Our friends in recovery will never scorn us if we fall short of any goal...other than the basic one: *"Don't use, and keep coming back."*

There is more reason for pride when we aim at a target and miss than there is when we shoot blindly and score a lucky bull's-eye or avoid taking aim at all. When fellow recovering addicts encourage us and refuse to let us be defeated by failure, we can always come back and try again.

"If our aim is to please everyone, we can expect failure. If some do not seek our friendship, we must not assume that they are enemies."

❖ *Acting and Reacting*

> *"Learning to act, not just react,*
> *is vitally important to our*
> *spiritual growth."*

Life in sobriety teaches us that we will
grow if we react to crisis and challenge
with a positive, spiritual attitude. When
we process our life experiences from a
spiritual point of view, we avoid mentally
reliving (and suffering) the events
preceding a painful experience. We
cannot alter many of the events and
circumstances that come into our lives.
What we can do, however, is gain control
over how we act in response to these
events and circumstances. Appropriate,
timely action will prevent outside
influences from taking control of our
emotions.

Simply stated, we learn to act instead of react when we study the principles of the Twelve Steps and practice them in all our affairs. With positive action, we can prove to ourselves that we *"intuitively know how to handle situations that used to baffle us."* When we develop more positive attitudes, we are more likely to act with composure and self-assurance. Only by taking appropriate and timely action can we deal with crisis and challenge effectively and bring positive change into our lives.

"Misfortune and good fortune are both part of the spiritual progress we make in our recovery program."

❖ *Backing Off*

> *"Those growing in recovery learn that happiness is not dependent upon winning every battle."*

While it might seem optimistic to believe that nothing is impossible, that attitude is unrealistic when battling an addiction by oneself. It is foolhardy to refuse to back off from certain defeat just to feel "heroic." We err further when we attempt to save face by continuing our pursuit of a lost cause. Backing off from confusion and chaos can help us buy valuable time with which to work out more rational and effective solutions to our problems.

There comes a time in the life of the active addict when he or she realizes that perhaps the battle for control over an addiction is an impossible battle to win. With that realization, the addict is likely to attend a Twelve Step meeting in a last ditch effort, so to speak, to find support and help.

"Recognizing and backing off from the impossible does not make us quitters. It is not how much we do, but how well we progress. When in doubt— pause, gather more information, and study the situation."

"Those who seek the height of human existence in sustained recovery and spiritual growth remember that first they touched the depths of despair."

Each cell in an organism works with all the other cells to insure its own survival and survival of the total organism as well. This same phenomenon seems to occur within us as we seek spiritual progress in a Twelve Step recovery program; we call this phenomenon *life force.* And the answers to why this phenomenon exists are with our Higher Power.

Awareness of the existence and power of a life force is the source of all inner strength. We must always keep ourselves open to a life force because it provides us with discernment, judgment, and clarity of understanding to know when to strive for goals and change—and when to let go. It is important to remember that in terms of our recovery, *we had to surrender before we could begin to win.*

"We cannot depend on our Higher Power to keep the channels open to our life force; that is our responsibility."

❖ *The A's That Score*

"We score a winning run by using The Four A's to advance from base to base."

Many recovering addicts discover that the use of analogies is helpful in expressing important insights and truths in recovery. *The Four A's* is an analogy that emphasizes the effectiveness of a one-step-at-a-time process of growth. *The Four A's* help the recovering addict see the importance of teamwork instead of the "heroics" of "I can do it myself; I don't need help." *The Four A's* also help the recovering addict see that steady progress, while not as spectacular as "the home run," is just as effective in winning.

Spiritual progress in recovery requires *Admitting* to reach first base; *Acceptance* to reach second base; *Application* of recovery principles to reach third base; and *Action* to reach home plate and victory.

"When we review our progress from one destination point to another, we are reminded that our program is based on One Day at a Time. Steady advancement is the surest way to victory."

❖ *False Friend*

> *"Our addiction gave us wings to fly, then took away the sky."*

In the early stages of our addiction, we actively sought out opportunities to use or act out—every holiday and anniversary, every success and failure came to represent just such opportunities. Later, our addiction became a "friendship," a "rescuer" we depended on in both adversity and good fortune. In time, our "fellowship" with addiction collapsed and we were in for a rude awakening: Dr. Jekyll became Mr. Hyde. In other words, a faithful friend and servant—our addiction— became a cruel master.

In the struggle for sobriety, our attitudes about our addiction changed. As we began to recover, we could see that our addiction was unmanageable, undesirable, and unnecessary. In recovery, we stop thinking about the "joys" related to our addiction. Then, in sobriety, we stop fixating on the fact that we can no longer use or act out. *With sustained sobriety, we find peace and freedom that enrich our lives forever.*

> "There are many roads to addiction, but only one path to recovery."

A Note from the Author

> *"There's a world of difference between reading the book* Alcoholics Anonymous *(the Big Book) and carefully studying that book."*

On this final page of reflections, I'd be remiss if I did not mention the many memorable and even life-saving words, phrases, sentences, paragraphs, and chapters that appear in the *Big Book*. This classic publication contains memorable help and inspiration for all recovering addicts and co-addicts, as well as family members, friends, advisors, helping professionals, and other interested people.

Cecil C.

Proof of Big Book study:

_____

*"If your copy of the Big Book is
tattered and torn, you can be sure
that the owner isn't."*

Topic Index